PUT IT IN PERSPECTIVE:
A Teen's Guide to Sanity

PUT IT IN PERSPECTIVE:
A Teen's Guide to Sanity

Kailen Krame

authorHOUSE®

AuthorHouse™ LLC
1663 Liberty Drive
Bloomington, IN 47403
www.authorhouse.com
Phone: 1-800-839-8640

Published by AuthorHouse   05/07/2014

ISBN: 978-1-4969-0276-4 (sc)
ISBN: 978-1-4969-0275-7 (e)

Library of Congress Control Number: 2014906266

Contents

Acknowledgements

When I first felt inspired to write this book at age sixteen, I never could have imagined that my ambitious dream to share my message would one day become a reality. I would like to express my gratitude and love to my family, whose support in both this book and in me has remained unyielding since the beginning. Thank you for all of your encouragement throughout the writing process, and for always having faith in me even when I didn't have it in myself. Dad, thank you so much for encouraging me to read the book that would ultimately transform my life. None of this would have been possible had you not introduced me to *Practicing the Power of Now,* which forced me to view life with a new perspective and inspired me to begin my journey of self-discovery.

Mom, I am beyond grateful for the countless hours we spent editing and re-editing my manuscript together in order to ensure that I arrived at a piece of work I could be proud of and that would properly spread my message. I also thank you for being my teacher and for always challenging me to deeply contemplate the unfolding mysteries of life. Simone, I would not have arrived at where I am today had it not been for your footsteps leading the way. Words cannot begin to describe how fortunate I feel to have you as a role model, and how much I appreciate your willingness to share your story with all the readers of this book. You are such an inspiration, and I can only hope that this book is just the beginning of our collaborative efforts to encourage others to view life with open hearts and minds.

In addition, writing this book would not have been possible without the support of Dwight-Englewood School and the mentorship of Mr. Kosnik. I am extremely grateful for all of the time you dedicated to guiding me throughout the writing process and serving the invaluable role as teacher, mentor, and friend. Lastly, thank you to Katherine Dieter for assisting with the final edit of my book and for helping me create a finished product that I am truly proud of.

Introduction

"Yesterday is gone. Tomorrow has
not yet come. We have only today.
Let us begin."—Mother Teresa

It was winter break of my sophomore year in high school, and I was away on vacation with my family. I lay in the tropical sun, its gentle rays caressing my skin and creating comforting warmth throughout my body. As I took in my picturesque surroundings, I began to feel both extremely calm and genuinely happy. This peaceful bliss was short-lived, however, and was soon replaced by a bout of panic and worry. Why had a wave of angst abruptly washed over me? It came with the daunting realization that I had not felt this calm, this carefree, this happy, in a very, *very*, long time.

Questions started to frantically pop into my head: When had the basic concepts of happiness and joy become foreign to me? Why hadn't I noticed sooner? And, more important, why was this happening to me at age fifteen? To try to answer these questions, I began to reflect on my life during the previous few months. My mind traveled backwards, searching for the one fateful event, specific date, or exact time when my happiness had slipped away.

I thoroughly racked my brain, but the specific answer I had been looking for—the one key that would unlock the secret door to my unhappiness—did not exist. There was no fateful event, specific date, or exact time that marked the moment I had lost myself. It had just happened at some point along the way, and I was too busy to notice it was gone. Too busy with the everyday stresses that plague the teenage years—schoolwork, boys, social life, family obligations, and all the rest—to notice that my true self had gotten lost among those pressures and that a stress-driven imposter had begun residing in its place.

Although it took me a while to notice the changes that had affected my well-being, I'm pretty sure my parents had realized that something about me was off. On this very same vacation, my father gave me a book to read called: *Practicing the Power of Now* by Eckhart Tolle, which preaches the importance of practicing mindfulness and living in the present moment. Hesitant at first (like all teens are when it comes to accepting suggestions from their parents), I started the book with little excitement and did not expect to get much out of it. As it would turn out, I couldn't have been more wrong. As I read on, the book's teachings seemed to deeply resonate with me, and, figuratively speaking, flipped a switch in my mind that would allow me to begin my journey of self re-discovery.

This journey, however, did not happen overnight. In the months following that moment of insight on my family vacation, the daily stresses continued, and I oftentimes found myself reverting back to my old habits and abandoning the new. It felt as if with every step I took forward, I would take two steps back. I tried repeatedly to put into practice what I had learned from the book my father had given me, but the stress had become so much a part of my identity that I no longer believed any methods could help me escape from it. It was as if I was living my life on autopilot, going from one thing to the next just trying to get by.

Throughout all of this mayhem I somehow managed to keep my grades up to par, although I sometimes felt I had to sell my soul, social life, and everything good just to get that all-important A. The stress to stay afloat was not only affecting my mental well-being, but it began to take a toll on other areas of my life as well. It had gotten to the point where I acknowledged the stress and allowed it to win temporarily, but I vowed that once the school year was over I would find myself again. So, when summer rolled around, I made it my mission to get my life back on track.

I viewed summer as an opportunity to leave my sophomore year behind, re-evaluate and re-claim my sanity, and start anew. Once the school year had ended and there were no deadlines to meet, exams to take, or places to be, I actually had *time* to think over things. I thought of my family vacation and the pivotal moment when I had noticed something wasn't right. I thought about the book I had read, how the teachings had resonated with me, and how I never had the time or frame of mind to implement them. I thought of myself, and of what I could do to help myself moving forward. Now that I had time to think, I realized I had two choices. I could continue living the way I had been and do everything as a means to an end, which would probably result in yet another treacherous year of school. On the other hand, I could make a conscious effort to live in the present moment and change my perspective, an effort that could ultimately help me deal with stress more appropriately in the upcoming school year. I chose the second option.

My conscious effort to be present in my everyday life eventually became second nature, and this optimistic outlook became the new lens through which I viewed every situation. Instead of being anxious about things in the future over which I ultimately had no control, I learned to enjoy every moment and calmly deal with any issue that came my way. I was no longer allowing my life to live me, but rather I was living it.

The purpose of this book is not for me to complain about the problems in my life, but rather to share with others the key to finding solutions to these problems. Almost all of you can relate to some aspect of my personal story, which creates the illusion that what all of us teens are experiencing is "normal." Once I became aware of this new of way thinking, however, I realized that what I experienced should in no way be characterized as "normal." How is it normal for someone to forget what happiness feels like, be overwhelmed by stress, and lose sight of who they are, all at the age of fifteen? The answer is simple: *it's not.*

It's one thing to be ambitious, but, in our fast-paced, competitive society, ambition has taken on a whole new meaning. The pressure to succeed has driven teens to the breaking point, causing them to burn out before they're even old enough to vote. Our lives are lives no longer, but rather constant competitions in which we must score the highest on our SATs, get into the best college, and graduate within the top 10% of our class, all the while making sure we act the right way in order to maintain our reputation and avoid potential bullying. In the midst of all this chaos disguised as a so-called "normal" teenage life, it is very easy to lose sight of who we are and brainwash ourselves into thinking that stress and unhappiness are just par for the course. This is, by no means, a healthy or proper way to live, and I seek to change this perspective.

Although I cannot eliminate any of the seemingly stressful situations in your everyday life, I can help you change the way you view them. In this book, I introduce you to various techniques that will help you to *"Put it in Perspective,"* and you will learn to embody five key qualities for staying sane throughout the high school years. I can only provide you with the tools necessary to live a happier, more meaningful life. What you choose to do with them is completely up to you.

In order to fully benefit from the teachings of this book and make a profound difference in your life, it is crucial that you have an open mind. If at times you are doubtful, refer back to my story. Always keep in mind that, unlike most "self-help" books geared towards teenagers, this one is not written by an adult whose teenage years were long ago, but is rather the voice of someone just like you. By no means do I wish to present myself as a big shot who knows all the answers. I simply discovered something that has worked for me and am sharing it with all of you in the hope that it will have the same effect. I, too, had a difficult time getting started, but, once I got a handle on things, I was able to create a happier and more meaningful lifestyle for myself. I compiled all that I had learned into a type of "philosophy"; it is now the means by which I live my everyday life, and it has changed my point of view. Once I discovered this "philosophy" and felt the positive influence it had on my life, I became eager to share it with all the kids out there like me. If I had found a new, better way to view the challenges in my life at such a young age, why couldn't other teens benefit as well? Thus, I decided that it would be much more beneficial for all you teenagers out there to learn from someone you could relate to; someone who had faced, and would continue to face, the same challenges that you do. So, consider us on this journey together. All you need is an open mind.

A NEW WAY TO THINK

Chapter 1: Getting Started

"We are the creators of our own destiny.
Be it through intention or ignorance, our
successes and failures have been brought
on by none other than ourselves."—
Enzo, The Art of Racing in the Rain

Before you can start to make changes in your life, you first need to identify what it is that you're looking to change. In order to begin the transition into a new approach to your life, it is important that you assess your life right now at this point in time. Take a moment to make a list of all the things in your life that you currently view as problems and want to change. There is nothing 'right' or 'wrong' that you can put on your list, just write down whatever enters your mind. At the back of this book you will find blank pages for you to do this exercise. This way, you can refer to this list at any point throughout your journey and use it as a point of reference.

After you make your list, look to see if your list is mainly composed of things that are more "emotional," or if it's composed of things that are more "circumstantial." An example of something "emotional" on your list might be: *"I am constantly anxious and want to feel calmer,"* whereas something "circumstantial" could be: *"I am assigned too much school work and have trouble getting it all done."* Recognizing the difference between the two is an important step in learning how to put things in perspective. You cannot control nor change many of the circumstances in your life; you can only control and change how you feel about them. Let's face it: for the rest of your life, you will continue to be confronted with problems and stressful situations. It sucks, but that's just how life is. The good news, however, is that most of what you seek to change— your feelings toward these problems and situations—is completely controlled by you. For instance, if you refer back to the examples mentioned earlier, you can see that feeling anxious is something you have control over and can work to change, whereas the amount of schoolwork you are given is not within your control. Therefore, in order to change the "circumstantial" problems in your life, you must change your emotional responses to them. Rather than resigning and feeling hopeless about the fact that you cannot change certain circumstances you are dealt, you can take an active role in changing how you view and feel about those circumstances.

Once you realize that you hold the solution within yourself, you can start to change your perspective. Dr. Wayne Dyer, a prominent author and speaker in the realm of self-development,

> You cannot control nor change many of the circumstances in your life; you can only control and change how you feel about them.

wrote in his book *The Power of Intention*: "Change the way

you view things and the things you view will change."
This phrase says something very profound: if you want to
change something in your life, all you need to do is change
the way you think or feel about it. Achieving and
maintaining this mindset is not an easy task, but, if you
focus whole-heartedly and practice what you learn, it can
eventually come to be your natural way of thinking. As
we move forward, we will explore this idea further and
learn more about how to take command of our emotional
responses.

"Change the way
you view things and
the things you view
will change."

Chapter 2: Happiness

"Happiness doesn't depend on any
external conditions; it is governed by our
mental attitude."—Dale Carnegie

"The purpose of our lives is to
be happy."—Dalai Lama

So far, we have only been focusing on what we want to change or eliminate from our lives (such as stress, anxiety, and negative emotional responses,) and have yet to even speak about the ultimate goal that we wish to obtain: *happiness*. In order to expel or reduce the feelings of stress and angst from our lives, we must change how we view the circumstances that cause them. Believe it or not, the same holds true for happiness. In order to be *truly* happy, we must alter our perception—and even our definition—of happiness and what we believe to be its source.

Similar to feelings of stress or angst, we associate feelings of happiness with physical things or circumstances. What I mean by this is that we tend to measure our happiness (or unhappiness) by objects, circumstances, and other people. Therefore, we have a misconstrued perception of happiness, instead of seeing it for what it really is: an emotion that *we,* and *we alone*, can control.

Think about how you're feeling right now: are you happy or unhappy? What happened today that made you feel this way? If you are someone who bases your happiness on an object, circumstance, or the thoughts and actions of other people, then your answer will most likely be related to an object, circumstance, or person. Are you happy today because you scored higher than your classmates on a test, or because you bought new clothes? Are you unhappy today because you failed a test, or because the boy/girl you like didn't even look your way?

If you allow external factors such as these to control your happiness, you will never experience true happiness. Yes, these things may seem important, but they are always temporary and fleeting, and therefore, if we let our happiness revolve around these things, our happiness, too, will be temporary and fleeting. The test that we aced today we could just as easily fail tomorrow, and the clothes we bought this week will no longer be new next week. These things are frequently changing, so it is impossible to expect real, long-lasting happiness from them. That is not to say that we cannot experience joy or sadness in the moments that these events occur, but they should not be the determiners of our happiness on a long-term scale.

As we will learn to do with stress, we also want to put our happiness in perspective. We can start by simply analyzing the things that make us happy, and then by identifying whether they are internally or externally driven. What this means is figuring out what controls your happiness. Is your happiness dependent upon external forces like a test grade, friend, etc? Or is your happiness derived from an internal source that you control? We generally experience a mix of both internal and external sources of happiness in our daily lives, but the goal is to shift towards having more internally based happiness. In his *"Wishes Fulfilled"* seminar, Dr. Wayne Dyer quoted an accomplished Bulgarian philosopher, Omraam Mikhaël Aïvanhov: "Instead of always waiting for their needs to be satisfied by some external force, human beings can absolutely work inwardly by means of their own thoughts, their own will, and their own spirit to obtain nourishing and healing elements that they need." Happiness is one of these nourishing, healing elements that we need. It is what we all strive for; and it is presumably why you are reading this book.

One problem that is all too common in our everyday lives is the power shift—we give other people, objects, and, circumstances the power to control whether we are happy, or unhappy, stressed out, or at ease. In the book *The Way*

To Love, by Anthony De Mello, the author discusses in detail this notion of temporary happiness brought about by material possessions (external) versus eternal happiness brought about by things of meaning (internal). De Mello describes the issue of the power shift by saying how our emotions are centered on these things we think we need (love, money, the approval of those in authority, etc.) and we are "happy" when we attain them, anxious when we don't, and upset when we lose them.

In this passage, De Mello perfectly captures the unjust amount of power we give to external things. If we are constantly waiting for things to make us happy and feeling anxious in the meantime, when will we ever be truly happy? By repeating false statements, such as: "I will be happy once I score higher on my SATs," you are not only giving unnecessary power and control to an inanimate object such as the SAT, but you are also putting your happiness on hold until a future date. If you don't end up scoring higher on the SAT, or even if you do, it's likely that statement will then become "I will be happy once I get into my top choice school," and so the pattern continues. If you keep waiting for something or someone else to make you happy, that happiness will never come; there will always be something better that you want or need shortly after. Therefore, the only way to achieve consistent happiness is to take the power back and keep it under your control. This, of course, takes time and practice, but by being aware of the difference between internally and externally driven happiness, and being conscious of how you feel, you have already taken the first step.

One common force that has the power to determine our happiness is stress. It's fairly straightforward: The less stress you have, the happier you feel, and vice versa. We know, therefore, that excessive stress is negative; and, in order to increase the happiness in our lives, we need to lessen our

> The less stress you have, the happier you feel, and the happier you feel, the less stress you have.

level of stress. Stress can negatively impact our lives on a social, psychological, and even physical level, and it is important that we do not allow stress to take over our lives and lay claim to our sanity. By incorporating certain tactics into our lives, we can work to change the way we think and feel about stress, and thus change the effect that it has on our minds and our bodies.

The methods that we are going to learn in this book are exclusively psychological, and they are geared towards changing the way you think—changing your perspective—about everyday circumstances and stressors. Some are specific coping mechanisms that you can apply to your everyday life, while others are mindsets or ways of thinking that can help you put things in perspective. These various methods, when combined, can help you develop a new way of thinking and put your mind and body at ease.

Remember:

- *Happiness is derived from an internal source that you control, not motivated by external factors.*

- *Don't fall victim to the **power shift** by giving other people, objects, and circumstances the power to control whether you are happy or unhappy, stressed-out or at ease.*

- *Don't put your happiness on hold until a future date: If you are constantly waiting for **things** to make you happy and feeling anxious in the meantime, when will you ever truly be happy?*

Chapter 3: Changing How We Think

"Few of us live in the present. We are forever anticipating what is to come or remembering what has gone."—Louis L'Amour

"Nothing in life is more remarkable than the unnecessary anxiety which we endure, and generally create ourselves."—Benjamin Disraeli

Learning tools to help you better cope with stress and other negative forces in your life is crucial to being a happy, well-adjusted person. The quote above by Benjamin Disraeli is one that I find to be extremely profound, and really gets to the heart of the message I wish to impart through this book. This quote places all the responsibility for how we feel on a day-to-day basis entirely on ourselves.

Rather than using circumstances as an excuse for why we may feel stressed or anxious, Disraeli is pointing out that how we think and feel is completely up to us. We can control how we think and react to certain situations; so therefore, we can control how we feel about them. It is reasonable to say that since we are the ones who cause most of our own suffering, we are the ones who can put a stop to it. Whether you are feeling anxious for a few days leading up to a test, or for an entire week after an unsettled argument with a friend, you can change how you feel about the situation simply through the power of your own thoughts.

This notion of controlling the way you think to affect the outcome of certain situations is a form of meta-cognition, or thinking about how you think. This may sound confusing, but basically all it means is that, in a given situation, you watch, then rationally analyze, what is going on in your mind. This term may be one that is new to you, but it can be applied to many different circumstances of your everyday life. For example, when you think about how you must train for sports and analyze different techniques, that process can be thought of as "meta-training." The idea is that you step outside of yourself and analyze what it is that you are doing, until doing it differently eventually becomes second nature. At the beginning of the season, you may need to review which technique works best or practice the basics, but, after you have examined those things and done them for a while, they start to become a part of how you operate. It becomes so natural that, in the game, you are no longer telling yourself "step right, left, right" to achieve perfect form, but

> We can control how we think and react to certain situations; so therefore, we can control how we feel about them.

rather you start doing it without even thinking. The same principle goes for metacognition; you must separate your thoughts into their different components before they can flow together as one. Just as you would repeat the phrase "right, left, right" until it became habit, you would repeatedly remind yourself of certain healthy ways to think until they became your natural way of thinking in given situations. The plus side to this idea is that we can change the way we think and feel, even if the circumstances do not change.

Our thoughts can cause us to feel certain emotions, which is why it is important for us to practice this "meta-cognition" (this "thinking about how we think"), and stop certain thoughts before they go haywire. What may start out in your mind as a reasonable concern can quickly evoke feelings of tremendous anxiety and worry if you start projecting into the future and allowing the "what ifs" to spiral out of control. One way to keep your thoughts and emotions in-check is through the practice of positive self-talk. Coincidentally, it is no different than it sounds: you talk to yourself in your mind. It might sound somewhat crazy, but it is easy and can be applied to any situation. An example of positive self-talk would be stopping to ask yourself (in your head): "In the scheme of my life, is this that big of a deal?" For most everyday circumstances, the answer is "no." This type of conversation allows you to step back for a second and put your current situation in perspective. By asking yourself this particular question or one that is similar, you are able to view your problems for what they are, and you catch yourself before you psychologically blow it out of proportion and get stressed out.

The aforementioned phrase "In the scheme of my life . . ." is one example of a method that can be initiated through positive self-talk. This is the idea of *perspective*: reminding yourself that what you are facing is small and insignificant in the greater scheme of things, and it will most likely not have as much of a bearing on your life in the big picture as you previously thought it would. This approach promotes rational thinking by taking a moment to prioritize your stressors and regain control over them.

At the onset of a stressful situation, a related concept of which to be aware is *mindfulness*. Being mindful means that you do not worry about what *could* happen in the future or what happened in the past, but rather analyze what is going on in this particular, present moment. Focusing on the breath can be a powerful tool for bringing your awareness back to the present moment, as well as reminding yourself to be present through positive self-talk. An example of mindful self-talk could be saying to yourself: "What's past is past; it already happened and is out of my control." Reminding yourself to be mindful will help you in circumstances when you are either regretful about something you might have done, or dreading something that may potentially happen in the future. Being mindful allows you to view the present moment: right *now,* in this very instant, is there anything to be worried about? If you break it down into a moment-by-moment replay, you will find that the answer to that question will almost always be "no."

The quote at the beginning of the chapter by author Louis L'Amour draws attention to the tendency for our minds to be everywhere but in the present. Once we become aware of this we can use mindful self-talk to calm ourselves and bring our consciousness back to the present moment. Although our bodies may physically be in the present moment, it is amazing how little time our minds actually spend there. Rather than living in the moment we are in, we are constantly planning for or thinking about another time. Taking a moment to draw oneself back to the present moment, though, has been proven to

Think about how you think.

have many benefits for both the mind and body. It is nearly impossible to feel stressed or anxious if you make a conscious effort to remain in the present moment. After all, how can you worry about things in the past and future if your mind is in the present? Remaining present cannot only help you feel better mentally and emotionally, but it can also change the way you act. In moments when we aren't being present, we tend to immediately get bent out of shape if something doesn't go our way because we start to think about everything that could continue to go wrong. When we are present during difficult times, however, we are able to assess the situation at face value, and think of a rational and appropriate way to take action. Therefore, it is important to keep this in mind when confronted with a stressful situation, as bringing yourself back to the present will help you to *respond* rather than *react.*

Another tool that you can use to help ease your stress is fairly simple and is something we do all the time: *breathe*. You have probably heard people instruct you to "just breathe" in stressful situations, but you are most likely unaware of just how powerful this simple practice can be, if done correctly. Focusing on your breathing not only helps you to relax, but it also allows you to take a moment to completely separate yourself from what you are doing and bring you into the present moment. When we are faced with stressors, our bodies experience an adrenaline rush. When our bodies are in

Be in this moment.

this heightened state, it is difficult to focus and address the task at hand (i.e. take a test, give a speech, etc.) By taking a deep, cleansing breath in that moment, you are allowing your body to calm down and restore its natural balance. Take a moment to try this now. Close your eyes and take three long, slow, deep breaths. How do you feel right now?

There are various types of breathing techniques that are more complex and will be covered later on in this book. For now, it is important that you simply learn to take slow, deep breaths in the midst of a stressful situation. When you breathe, really focus on inhaling and exhaling, and take as many breaths as you need until you feel as though you have calmed down and can approach the situation with a fresh state of mind. Breathing may sound easy, since we do it all the time without even thinking about it, but it takes practice in order for it to calm you down effectively. Therefore, instead of trying to use it for the first time when you are under stress and expecting it to work, start by practicing it throughout the day at times when you are relatively calm (in the car, at your desk in school, in the shower, etc.) Setting aside a few minutes each day to practice this method when you are not in a panicky or anxious state of mind will allow you to get familiar with this coping technique and perfect it. Then, when you find yourself in a stressful situation, you will instinctively know what to do and better your chances of employing the method effectively.

If you have never been introduced to positive self-talk, mindfulness, or breathing techniques before, they may seem strange at first and a little difficult to incorporate into your life on a daily basis, but don't give up—it really helps! In the next section of this book, I will expand upon these ideas, and you will learn how to incorporate these methods into your everyday life by embodying five important qualities: acceptance, compassion, selfishness, resilience and fearlessness.

Remember:

- *Positive self-talk: Keep your thoughts and emotions in check by talking to yourself in your mind.*
- *Keep things in perspective: Remind yourself that what you are facing is small and insignificant in the greater scheme of things.*
- *Be mindful: Don't worry about what could happen in the future or what happened in the past. Rather, pay attention to what is going on right **now** in this particular, present moment.*
- *Respond rather than react.*
- *Use your breath as a tool to separate yourself from what you are doing and to bring yourself into the present moment.*

FIVE QUALITIES
FOR MAINTAINING SANITY

Chapter 4: Acceptance

"It's not a matter of letting go—you would if you could. Instead of 'Let it go,' we should probably say 'Let it be.'"—Jon Kabat-Zinn

The first quality you must embody in order for you to be able to implement mindfulness into your everyday life and change your perspective is *acceptance*. Acceptance is the first step to changing how you live your life, since it allows you to embrace each situation as it is, rather than use judgment or resistance, both of which are stressful. When we are presented with a situation we are not familiar with, our initial reaction is to either pass judgment or resist. Rather than accepting each situation for what it is, our fear drives us to immediately be on the defensive.

We spend so much of our time trying to avoid or change what is right in front of us, when we would be better off simply accepting what is and "let it be." Using judgment and resistance are ways of driving yourself further from the present, since you are denying what is true and real in that moment.

Being judgmental is one of the worst things we can do, yet we do it all the time. Whether we are meeting someone for the first time or presented with a question on an exam, we always use judgment as a way to make sense of things that are new. Instead of simply accepting the person or test question in front of us, we use our judgment to label or categorize them as either good or bad, easy or hard.

In order to view things with a better perspective, it helps to view each situation in a neutral way, rather than immediately labeling it as either good or bad, right or wrong, etc. After all, judging the person you meet as being "overbearing" or labeling the question on the exam as "difficult" is not going to change what is right in front of you, and is only going to evoke feelings of discomfort and unease.

Having acceptance is also extremely important in regards to yourself. Self-acceptance is the foundation of stable and healthy relationships, since the relationship we have with ourselves tends to be reflected in our relationship with others. There are many characteristics and personality traits that each person wishes they could change about themselves, but the key to happiness is to accept the things we cannot change. Some things are simply out of our control, and resisting this idea rather than coming to terms with it is only going to cause pain and suffering. It is important, however, to understand that acceptance is not the same as resignation. With things you actually have control over, such as your behavior or how you interact with others, you can and should make a conscious effort to change it for the better rather than resigning and saying, "That's just how I am." With things you wish to change but do not have control over, such as your height or a sudden skin break-out, being able to accept yourself the way you are will grant you strength and inner peace in the long run.

When you accept the circumstances you are handed in life rather than resist them, you will find that you feel much more at ease and have less tension. If you are unhappy with your circumstances, you should of course try to change them, but it is acceptance, rather than resistance or denial, that will allow you to make the changes you desire. With mindfulness, one key idea is to realize that things have already happened, and therefore it is important to forgive yourself or the circumstances and move on, rather than dwell on past events that cannot be changed. So, if you are holding a grudge against yourself or someone else over something you cannot control, try to let it go. Once you start to acknowledge *what is* rather than try to judge, resist, label, or harp on it, you have started on the path towards acceptance.

When people have trouble accepting themselves and others, problems such as bullying, peer pressure, and depression arise. Constantly resisting everything that comes your way will only give you a life full of tension and struggles, whereas having the courage to accept things as they are will allow you to be happier and more at peace. Resistance and judgment are at the root of so many problems, and all it takes to resolve both the internal and external conflicts we endure is acceptance.

When you are dealing with certain issues it may feel as though it is impossible to break the cycle and start to change, but it can be done—I have witnessed it happen firsthand. I have a sister who is four years older than me, and we have always been very close growing up. However, for the majority of her teenage years I watched with heartbreak as my sister dealt with issues of insecurity, anxiety, and depression. To the outside world, she was an outgoing, happy person, but on the inside she felt insecure and was unhappy with herself. Although she did her best to conceal it, her inner conflict worked itself into other aspects of her life and impacted how she related to and interacted with others. She worked on changing and even thought that she was practicing mindfulness, but now that she has actually overcome her issues and has altered her perspective, she realizes that there was a mental and physical disconnect that prohibited her from being able to truly be mindful. She had been dealing with these issues for so long, it was as if part of her didn't want to change; she had grown accustomed to being unhappy and didn't believe it was possible to fully overcome everything. It's ironic—her discomfort began to feel like somewhat of a comfort, since it was what she was familiar with and she didn't know any other way. For years she was trapped in this troubled state: as soon as one problem was solved, another one arose. It wasn't until she started to gain full acceptance and view things from a different perspective that she was able to implement the practices of mindfulness and make a change, as she shared with me:

"I used to say that I am the most compassionate, loving person to everyone except myself. I couldn't comprehend why I always put myself down. When I started accepting myself for how I am, not how I thought I should be, my life changed. Although no one else would have known that I was insecure and lacked self confidence, the moment I changed, the vibes I sent out must have been different because people started reacting to me differently. Random strangers began to engage me in conversation. I realized that it really is true that if you love yourself, others will as well."

As with a lot of teenagers, most of my sister's insecurities related to her physical appearance. For years she battled severe acne, which dealt a serious blow to both her self-image and self-confidence. She would blame herself and beat herself up over something that was out of her control, and she allowed her skewed perception of herself to influence how she acted around others. Outwardly, she was warm and friendly, but in her mind she was always worried that people were judging her and focusing on her flawed skin.

In today's society there is a huge emphasis on physical appearance, and it is no wonder why many of us struggle with issues of self-consciousness and insecurity. Thanks to television and magazines, we are constantly bombarded with airbrushed images of stick-thin, tall, bronzed beauties alongside perfectly toned men who look as though they were chiseled out of marble. It's a bit overwhelming . . . and absurd. Because it is nearly impossible to escape these constant reminders of "beauty," we tend to think less of ourselves, as if we are not good enough if our physical appearance fails to meet the high standards set by society. Even if it isn't celebrities who we aspire to look like, we tend to compare ourselves to our friends and those around us and feel the pressure to keep up.

People even go to the extreme of harming themselves if they are not satisfied with what they see in the mirror, but why give something such as physical appearance the reins to control you? *You* need to stay in control, rather than give control to the superficial demands of society. You are who you are, unique in your own way. I am a firm believer in the notion that if you exude confidence and are sure of yourself, that is what draws others towards you and makes you attractive. You may feel as though it is hard to be confident if you do not think of yourself as being attractive, but there is more to being attractive than your physical appearance. True beauty goes deeper than that.

If you know someone who is attractive physically and appears to be confident but is rude or malicious in their interactions with other people, they are most likely insecure inside. It is not beauty that makes confidence; it is self-acceptance. Even the most beautiful people may not be confident or accepting of themselves, and as a result, it affects how they interact with others. For those of you who keep up with American pop culture, you can probably quote the movie *Mean Girls* from start to finish, or, at the very least, have watched it once or twice. It may be a bit of an exaggerated example, but the movie still exemplifies the importance of confidence that stems from self-acceptance rather than beauty. The mean girls in the movie are pretty, but are nasty towards others. Although their attractive physical appearance gives the illusion that they are confident, their malicious behavior actually stems from an underlying insecurity. If they were truly accepting of themselves, they would not feel the need to put others down to elevate their sense of self-worth. From this example, or perhaps from real examples you have seen in your own life, it is important to realize that confidence and physical beauty should not always be linked together, nor is one dependent on the other.

Once you have realized that confidence is the result of self-acceptance rather than beauty, you can stop

> Confidence is the result of self-acceptance.

putting so much emphasis on physical appearance. If you obsess over trying to change your physical appearance and keep harping on it, you will never be happy. Trying to change your appearance is a quick fix and can only grant you temporary joy. What you really need to change is your level of self-acceptance. You can change the way you look and tell yourself you are happy, but if you are not accepting of yourself, it will only be a matter of time before that "happiness" runs out and you are looking for something else to fix. Being this critical of yourself will eventually drive you insane. If you want to be truly confident and have security in your relationship with both yourself and others, you must learn to accept yourself the way you are. Your physical appearance can still be something that is important to you, but it need not be what determines your happiness:

"In the past, I was never truly happy because I placed so much emphasis on unimportant things—mainly having to do with my physical appearance. It was like the minute one problem was solved I found another one to focus all my attention on and the self-pity started all over again.

As a result I never fully enjoyed all the good things in my life and let many precious moments slip away. Through my experience, I have finally learned that if you are unhappy with your appearance, you must be kind to yourself, rather than beat yourself up, in order for anything to change.

I finally understand that although there are always going to be things going on in my life that aren't perfect, I cannot let them dictate my happiness. Now, whenever I feel like I am reverting to my old way of thinking, I remember to focus on what's really important, and in doing so, I am reminded that I have so much good in my life and have the power to control my happiness."

My sister's insecurity drove her to become her own worst critic, especially when it came to her physical appearance. She is a beautiful girl but her lack of confidence convinced her otherwise. She got so caught up with trying to fix her physical appearance that she missed out on opportunities in other aspects of her life. It was not until she began to accept herself that she was able to become truly confident and see herself the way everybody else did: self-assured, outgoing, and beautiful. Once she put things in perspective and realized what was truly important in life, she gave superficial things such as her physical appearance less power, and in turn gained control of both her happiness and her life.

Changing your perspective may take time— be patient and persistent!

I'm sharing my sister's story with you because it is one of both inspiration and hope. My sister is not any more important than each and every one of you. In fact, she is just like you. Her story serves as an example to show that it may take awhile to obtain self-acceptance and finally change your perspective—it took her years!—but it *is* possible. Watching my sister go through such a tough time and then eventually being able to overcome it served as an inspiration for this very book. There were many times when she doubted herself and thought things would never work out for her, but she remained persistent until she eventually had a breakthrough. By using tools such as mindfulness and positive self-talk, she was able to let go of her past, accept herself for who she is, and reach a new, stable point in her life. If you ever doubt yourself, think back to my sister's story and remember that, no matter how difficult it might seem, you *can* make a change!

Remember:

- *Embrace each situation as it is, rather than judging or resisting.*
- *It is not physical beauty that gives you confidence; it's self-acceptance.*

Chapter 5: Compassion

"You can search throughout the entire universe for someone who is more deserving of your love and affection than you are yourself, and that person is not to be found anywhere. You, yourself, as much as anybody in the entire universe, deserve your love and affection."—Buddha

Once you have achieved some level of acceptance, the next characteristic necessary for changing how you live is *compassion*. We have established that being able to accept both yourself and the circumstances in your life will help you be more at peace, yet this cannot be fully accomplished without compassion. To have compassion is to accept things the way they are, and then be able to respond with kindness. In a sense, compassion and acceptance go hand-in-hand, as you will not be able to truly accept things the way they are if you do not have compassion and understanding.

With many of the challenges we are faced with during the teenage years, it is important that we remain kind to ourselves. When the going gets rough we tend to be especially hard on ourselves, but this does not make any situation easier. Therefore, in times of struggle, we might as well practice compassion and be kinder to ourselves instead of adding fuel to the fire.

We are the ones who set our own expectations for ourselves, and therefore we become our own worst critics when we fail to meet them. We do, of course, have parents and teachers who also do the job, but we are the ones who ultimately set our own standards. Having high expectations for yourself is good because it generates persistent and determined behavior, but it has a downside as well. Because we make up our own expectations, we in turn manufacture worry upon ourselves. We must get an A on the test, and therefore, before the test has even begun, we are already worrying about the consequences if we score anything less. It is one thing to be driven, but we need not allow our expectations to drive us. It is our loss of control over these expectations that induces a feeling of panic, which is why we must make a conscious effort to stay in control and treat ourselves with more compassion. If, from the beginning, we put less pressure on ourselves, we can prevent feelings of disappointment or failure down the road. What this basically means is: why be the cause of our own problems if, instead, we can prevent them simply by having more compassion for ourselves?

Whether dealing with your academic performance or physical appearance, you can make an effort to bring compassion into each area of your life. High school has become an increasingly competitive environment, and the desire to do well and get into a good college has forced many students to forget to have compassion for themselves. When on the quest for success, it is important to distinguish between ultimatums and goals. An example of an ultimatum would be "I *must* get an A on this exam or I won't get into college," whereas a goal would be "I am going to work hard to get an A." When you set an ultimatum for yourself, the voice in your head is one of a demanding tyrant, whereas when you set goals for yourself, the voice is more encouraging and nurturing.

We obviously want to do our best, but in the event that we do not meet our own expectations, we will feel a lot worse about ourselves if we are motivated by ultimatums rather than goals. It is one thing to strive to get good grades and feel proud when we do so, but the grades we receive should not be measures of our self-worth.

> Be driven, but don't let your expectations drive you.

If we begin to identify ourselves with the grades we achieve, we will eventually view ourselves as little more than a number. This number constantly fluctuates, and, therefore, if we base our sense of self on this number, the way we view ourselves will fluctuate too.

Chances are, most of us have been taught the Golden Rule: Treat others the way you want to be treated. This, of course, is an example of compassion, but it needs to work the other way around as well: I treat myself the way I want others to treat me. We wouldn't want others to judge, ridicule, belittle, or have unrealistic expectations of us, so why do it to ourselves? With everything that we have going on at school and in our social lives, the last thing we need is added pressure coming from ourselves. Being kinder to yourself will help reduce stress and allow you to treat others more kindly as well.

The idea of being kinder to yourself and setting goals rather than ultimatums is one that can be applied to all areas within the academic realm. As you get older and work your way up the high school totem pole, it may seem as though the pressure increases with each year. Once the infamous junior year rolls around and you are faced with college talk and standardized testing, it is especially important that you have compassion for yourself.

Even before registering for standardized tests, many teens have an idea about where they see themselves going to college. For those who set ultimatums for themselves, rather than goals, the desire to go to a specific university can turn into something destructive. When these students become steadfast on attending one school and no other, they not only put extreme pressure on themselves, but they also skew their perspective on the entire college process. I think of those people who have convinced themselves that X University is the *only* place for them as viewing the college process with tunnel vision. They have a narrow view of what they want, and refuse to believe that anything outside of their tunnel is acceptable or can make them happy. Well, if they keep telling themselves this, it will start to become true. If they ultimately do not get into X University, they will blame themselves for not being good enough and feel as if they will be "settling" for another school. This can, and often does, adversely affect their experience at that school. Rather than having tunnel vision, it helps to maintain the mentality of "everything happens for a reason." It may sound a bit corny, but I truly believe that if you work hard, are kind to yourself, and keep an open mind, you will end up where you belong. The college process is one big crapshoot, and if things do not turn out as you expected they would, it is important to have compassion rather than get down on yourself over a decision that you had no control over. If you view your college application process in this way, you are no longer setting an ultimatum for yourself or creating narrow boundaries for your happiness.

Looking back at my own experience, I can honestly say that having compassion and kindness for myself is what kept me grounded throughout the college selection process. I initially convinced myself that there was one particular school that was right for me, and applied Early Decision with full confidence that I would be admitted. I really wanted to attend this university, and during the months that I waited for my decision, I tried to remain calm and have compassion for myself rather than create unnecessary stress and pressure. At times when I felt anxious, I would use positive self-talk to help keep things in perspective and would say things such as: "It is what it is, everything happens for a reason. I want to attend this school, but if they do not accept me, then it was not meant to be and I will be happy somewhere else." My friends commended me for being so calm and collected, and repeatedly assured me that I was definitely going to be accepted to my first choice university.

Sure enough, when decisions were released in December, I did not get in to this "dream school" of mine. I felt upset and shocked for a moment, but was able to bounce back almost immediately once I reminded myself of the attitude I had maintained while awaiting my decision. Many people would have taken this decision personally and would have been disappointed in themselves, but having compassion for myself is what allowed me to find peace with the situation. Getting down on myself would not have changed the outcome, so I might as well have been positive, which helped me cope with the difficult news. I maintained this attitude throughout the college process, and ultimately ended up at the perfect school for me. I got into the sorority I wanted to, made some amazing new best friends, love my classes and professors, and honestly, could not be any happier. Friends who follow me on Facebook are constantly remarking how much fun I seem to be having. While attending a recent gathering of my high school graduating class, I found that many of my friends and classmates seemed to be unhappy with their "dream schools" and are thinking about transferring; which is okay, but it is important to keep an open mind and remember that there is more than just "one" particular school that is right for you. Applying to college may be a stressful and daunting experience, but if you have compassion and remain positive throughout the process, you will be much better off.

The same holds true in regards to physical appearance. In the last chapter, we discussed the societal pressure to look a certain way and learned how self-acceptance plays a crucial role in being able to relieve this pressure. The story that I shared about my older sister exemplifies the importance of having self-acceptance, but it also demonstrates the need for self-compassion. We tend to be our own worst critics, and when we discover a perceived flaw in our physical appearance or personality, we are usually quite unforgiving. Once we find something about ourselves that we do not like, we can easily focus on it and allow it to consume us. You wouldn't want someone else to tell you that your thighs are too big or that your teeth are slightly crooked, so why is it acceptable when the voice in your head is the one constantly repeating these things? It is amazing to think of how much pain and suffering could be avoided if the person staring back at us in the mirror had a bit more compassion.

If you have found some self-acceptance with your perceived flaws, the next step is to be kind to yourself, rather than resentful. There are many negative, hateful people that you are going to encounter in your lifetime, so why be your own enemy when you can be your own ally? You spend more time

Be your own ally.

with yourself than you do with anyone else, so you might as well be good company. Being critical of yourself only causes more stress and tension, while being compassionate and supportive will allow you to view each situation in your life in a happier, more optimistic way.

Remember:

- *Compassion: The ability to accept things the way they are and respond with kindness.*
- *Set goals and objectives rather than ultimatums.*
- *Treat yourself the way you want others to treat you.*

Chapter 6: Selfishness

*"To be yourself in a world that is
constantly trying to make you something
else is the greatest accomplishment."—
Ralph Waldo Emerson*

With acceptance and compassion being the first two qualities necessary for thriving in high school, it may be a bit surprising to see selfishness on the list. Upon hearing the word "selfish," we tend to think of people who put themselves first and do not care about the needs of others. I am not encouraging you to disregard others' needs, but the aspect of selfishness that I think is extremely important to embody throughout the teenage years is to put yourself first.

With the desire to fit in teenagers often place a lot of importance on what is good for everybody else, rather than consider what is best for themselves. We are often so concerned about what everybody else says and thinks that we disregard our own thoughts and beliefs. Compromising personal beliefs for the sake of fitting in can lead teenagers to do some pretty terrible things that they normally would not do.

The use of drugs and alcohol is the most common example, but not the only one, of how peers influence one another. Whether it is the decision to shoplift or the choice to partake in bullying a fellow student, any time that your actions are performed to impress others is considered peer pressure. In regard to this, my philosophy has always been to be selfish. When presented with the opportunity to follow the crowd in doing something you don't want to do, put yourself first. Make a decision based on what is best for *you,* not what is best for others.

This can be applied to your actions towards others, but it should also be taken into account with regard to yourself. Many teenagers try to present themselves in a certain way because they want others to like them, but the single most important thing is whether or not you like yourself (self-acceptance). Rather than

> Put yourself first.

worrying about which style of clothing will make you look cooler or whether or not your taste in music is similar to everyone else's, stay true to your own interests and beliefs. Presenting yourself in the "right way" to others may grant you short-term popularity, but staying true to yourself and doing what feels right for you will be much more valuable and rewarding in the long run.

Staying in control and assuming power over your life are two concepts that are of utmost importance throughout the high school years. Although we may not all be the alpha dog in our social group, it is important that we remain strong, independent individuals. All of us are fully capable of making our own decisions and doing what is best for us, so why give someone else the power to control what we say and do? The next time you find yourself in a position where you are forced to do something you don't want to do, think about it this way: you do what works for you, and if others aren't okay with that, that is their problem, not yours. It may sound a bit harsh, but at the end of the day, you will be much better off if you listen to yourself rather than if you do things for the sole purpose of pleasing others.

Many people are inclined to give in to peer pressure because they fail to see the consequences of their actions in the big picture. We tend to view our actions in a narrow way and only take the immediate results into account, oftentimes ignoring what effects they might have in the long run. The belief that we teens are invincible causes us to make decisions with the mindset of "it can't happen to *me*," but the truth of the matter is that it always happens to *someone.* By allowing others to make your decisions for you, you are increasing the chances of that 'someone' eventually being you. When peer-pressure puts you in a tough situation, take a moment to ask yourself: what is it worth? When answering, you will come to see that the response of "I want to look cool in front of my friends" is quite a foolish one. After all, you are the one who has to live with the consequence of your actions, not your friends. Taking a moment to put things in perspective will not stop peer pressure, but rather, it will allow you to view it differently and regain control of the situation.

Don't make split-second decisions— be mindful.

One of the most pressing issues regarding peer pressure is the feeling of powerlessness and loss of control. When others call the shots for us, we feel as though we have lost control over the situation and are forced to do as they say. When faced with a tough decision, it is important that you remember to be mindful. Rather than make a split-second decision, take a step back and carefully view the situation. If you take a minute to analyze the circumstances and view them from a new perspective, you will see that you have the option to take charge rather than giving others the power to make your decisions. If you remain strong and have the courage of your convictions, you will be the one who has control over the situation, and it will no longer matter whether someone else agrees with your choice or not.

The topic of drugs and alcohol seems to be a touchy one to discuss within the teenage community. You have to remember that I, too, am a teen and hate it when people try to lecture me about these things. So, this isn't a lecture. I am going to give you a few things to think about, and you do with them what you will.

The teenage years are a time of discovery and along with this comes experimentation. We are curious and want to try new things, and for some that includes drugs and alcohol. The reasons why teens choose to use drugs and alcohol vary, but the one that is most common is that "everyone is doing it."

As we discussed in the chapter about acceptance, the way that people interact with others is influenced by their relationship with themselves. People who are insecure or are not very accepting of themselves may be more inclined to follow the crowd and base their decisions on what others think. If you have used drugs and alcohol or are thinking about it, take a moment to ask yourself: "Why do I use/want to use drugs and alcohol?" Your answer will most likely include reasons that involve other people, rather than yourself. It may be because a friend has coaxed you into trying it, or maybe you willingly tried it and never thought anything of it because others were doing it as well. The decision to use drugs and alcohol almost always relates back to other people in one way or another, and very rarely is it the case that people do it solely for themselves. The solution to this problem is one that has been stated before in this section: *be selfish*.

Take the power back into your own hands and don't allow other people to make your decisions for you. When dealing with something that can be very harmful to you, like drugs and alcohol, why put the power in someone else's hands? The consequences of using substances can be severe, and putting yourself in potential danger just to please others is simply not worth it. I'm not telling you not to drink or try drugs since it's not my place to preach to you; however, take a moment to think about why you're doing it, how often you're doing it, and in what set of circumstances.

Whether it is drinking because a friend pressures us or because we want to "let our guards down" in uncomfortable social settings, the decision to drink often originates from the desire to please others. A person may not read that far into it in the moment that they are funneling a beer or taking a shot, but this desire still exists whether they are consciously aware of it or not. If someone is feeling insecure, they may reach for a drink impulsively as a way to feel more comfortable conversing and interacting with others. This mindset is a self-limiting one, however; people convince themselves that they "need" a few drinks in their system in order to socialize. If teenagers didn't convince themselves that the *only* way to have fun is when drugs or alcohol is involved, then that wouldn't be the case. Unfortunately, a friend of mine learned this the hard way:

Emily went to a party hosted by a friend of hers. She was feeling insecure and wanted to let loose, so she decided to take some shots. After a few shots it began to go to her head, and she was having a good time and making her friends laugh. Her judgment was clouded, and she continued to drink until she lost track of how many drinks she had had. She does not remember the rest of the evening. She got violently sick and passed out unconscious, and was completely unresponsive to all of her friends' attempts to take care of her. Her friends called one of her parents to take her to the hospital, and shortly thereafter the police arrived at the house to bust up the party.

The next morning Emily woke up in a hospital bed without any recollection of what had happened the night before. The doctors informed her that if she had had just one more drink, she would probably have died of alcohol poisoning. Just like that—just one more drink! The following Monday at school her episode was the main topic of conversation, and she was ridiculed by all of her friends for making a bad decision and ruining the party.

A few days later I spoke to her about what happened, and, although she was not entirely sure of what she had done, she was still clearly ashamed of her actions. When I asked her why she decided to drink that much, she confided in me that she feels extremely insecure in social environments, and that drinking alcohol is the only way for her to feel comfortable and as if she belongs. Emily was disappointed in herself, and, for the weeks following the incident, she could not stop dwelling on what had happened and beating herself up about the poor choices she had made.

The choices that Emily made that night were not entirely decided by her, but rather by her insecurities. She felt awkward at the party and looked to alcohol to help make her feel more relaxed and sociable. The decision to have the first drink may have seemed harmless at first, yet from there she drank excessively until she lost control and could not stop. When she poured herself her first drink that evening, she was not thinking of what could—and did—happen to *her*, but rather, her main concern was being part of the crowd. From Emily's story we can learn a valuable lesson about peer pressure and alcohol. Emily was driven to drink by her insecurities and the pressure she placed on herself to appear "cool" in front of her friends. Actually, it was not her peers who forced her to drink, but rather her own insecurities and desire to fit-in. As a result, Emily put herself in a life-threatening situation. So, the next time you are in an environment when drugs and alcohol are present, ask yourself: "Do I really want to be doing this?" "Why am I doing this?" It is important that you think things through and really know the answer before you get yourself into what could be a potentially dangerous situation.

When I spoke with Emily shortly after this incident had occurred, I gave her guidance not unlike the advice I have provided here in this book. Among other things, I addressed the feelings of disappointment and self-loathing she felt about her actions. I stressed to her the concepts of mindfulness, compassion, and self-acceptance, and I reminded her that although she may have used poor judgment, it was in the past and there was no longer anything she could do to change the situation. I also reminded her that the only thing she could do *now*, after the fact, was to try to put the situation behind her and avoid making the same mistake twice. There was no point in getting upset about and dwelling over what she had already done, since her actions could not be undone, despite how much she wished they could be. I remember talking to her as we sat at a table in Starbucks:

Me: *Is there anything right here, right now, for you to be upset over?*

Emily: *Yeah, I completely messed everything up. I was so stupid and now my friends are mad at me and my parents are mad at me.*

Me: *No. I mean, right now. Sitting here drinking your coffee. Is there anything about this moment to make you upset?*

She gave me a confused look.

Emily: *Well . . . no. But—*

Me: *Exactly. I understand that you made a bad decision, but getting upset about it is not going to change the situation. You still did it. It's over with, and you cannot change that, so there's no point in reliving it and making yourself miserable. Acknowledge that you are ashamed of what you did, promise yourself you will never do something like this again, and then forgive yourself. It'll be much easier to move on and change if your regrets and embarrassment aren't weighing you down.*

The advice that I gave to Emily relates back to the concepts of self-acceptance and compassion, the two qualities Emily needed most of all in this situation. It was her insecurity that got her into trouble in the first place, so in order to avoid going down the same path again, it was crucial that she forgave herself. If you have been in a situation such as Emily's before, or if something like this happens to you in the future, it is important that you forgive your actions and are accepting of yourself. Just as you wouldn't want your friend to hold a grudge when you're truly sorry, you should not hold a grudge against yourself. I am not trying to minimize the severity of Emily's actions, or any similar situation, but I think it is important that you try to move on rather than constantly reliving the event in your mind. When you experience something like this, there are two ways that you can learn from it. You can allow your shame, fear, and embarrassment to get the better of you and damage your relationship with yourself, or, you can allow your shame, fear, and embarrassment to empower you to get your act together and improve. If you choose the first option, you will only worsen any issues with self-acceptance and insecurity, which increases the chances of you getting involved in a similar situation, or one that is worse. If you opt for choice number two, rather than ruminating over your mistakes, you will be able to turn your negative situation into a positive one and grow to be a better person.

By choosing to be self-accepting rather than self-denigrating, you can transform those feelings

> Don't hold a grudge against yourself: forgive yourself.

of shame, fear, and embarrassment into ones of confidence, strength, and security. Obviously the hope would be that none of you ever find yourself in this situation, but realistically it could happen to any one of us, which is why it is important to address the proper way to deal with it when it happens. It is unrealistic to say that you should never, ever try drugs or alcohol during the teenage years. However, if there is one thing I wish to emphasize it is to really, truly think things through before you make decisions to please others. *It's okay to be selfish.*

Remember:

- *It's okay to be selfish: put yourself first.*
- *Make decisions based on what is best for you, not what is best for others.*

Chapter 7: Resilience

"Happiness is not the absence of problems but the ability to deal with them."—H. Jackson Brown

"When one door of happiness closes, another opens; but often we look so long at the closed door that we do not see the one which has been opened for us."—Helen Keller

Once you have worked on acceptance, compassion, and are able to put yourself first (selfishness), the next quality that will help you cope with the teenage years is *resilience.* To be resilient is to have the courage and strength to let go of your problems and move on. Resilience and mindfulness are inextricably linked, since the focus of mindfulness is to be present and rid yourself of anything that does not serve you in the current moment. Resilience is crucial during the teenage years; you will be better able to plan for future success if you are not burdened by past problems or failures.

Resilience can be applied to any area of your life where you may experience obstacles, such as school work, social life, self-esteem, sports, and so on. Everybody faces bumps in the road, but it is crucial to move past the difficult times and learn from them, rather than allowing them to be repeated in the future. As stated in the example with Emily, when something undesirable happens to us it is imperative that we *let it go*, and *let it be*. How you deal with the situation as it arises is extremely important as well, but if you remain hung-up on it after the fact, the actions you took to cope along the way are ultimately futile. If you find yourself fixating on an incident after it has passed, practicing mindfulness can help you regain control. By saying: "It has already passed, there is nothing I can do about it now," or asking yourself: "Is there anything right *now* in this moment to be worried about?" you will be able to return to the present moment, rather than reliving a past event and experiencing the accompanying angst and worry.

Take a moment to really think about it: Once something has happened, is there really anything you can do to change it? No, it has already been done, and unless you have a time machine, you cannot undo it. Therefore, instead of beating yourself up about something you cannot change, work on changing the things you can at this point in time. Once you become aware of this truth and whole-heartedly believe it, you will be able to face problematic situations in a completely new and rational way. Once we have put the past in perspective, we can move on to the other part of mindfulness, which is putting the present in perspective. Simply asking: "Is there anything right now in this moment to be worried about?" is a way to isolate yourself from a problem of the past and assure yourself of the fact that you are no longer presented with it. Once you realize that what happened is no longer happening or within your control, you will see that it is foolish to remain bothered by it or to allow it to interfere with your present and future.

Part of being resilient is to never take things personally. When we make mistakes or don't perform at our best, we tend to blame ourselves and view them as flaws in our character. When we do something wrong, we should, of course, take responsibility for our actions, but when we make a one-time mistake we should not let it impact how we view ourselves moving forward. Rather than dwelling on your mistakes and watching them on instant replay in your mind, try to replace negative thoughts with positive ones. You can do this through creative visualization, which is trying to envision a successful outcome in your mind. Here's how: Picture in your mind a result that you want, and try to vividly see yourself achieving that result. Rather than replaying bad moments over which you no longer have control, work towards making your mental goals and visualizations a reality, which is something you *do* still have control over. Picture the end result exactly as you want it to be. Really see it in your mind.

While you want to experience resilience after your own actions or mistakes, it is incredibly important that you also demonstrate resilience in regard to others' actions towards you. When somebody says something hurtful or treats you badly, it is easy to allow their actions to put a dent in your self-esteem. If you practice self-acceptance and compassion, however, it will be much easier for you to be resilient and not take their insults personally. There will always be others who make negative comments or try to knock us down in life, but that is *their* problem, not yours. A "friend" approaches you and says: "What an ugly shirt," or "You're new haircut doesn't look good." Granted, your first reaction is to be hurt and you might even be a little embarrassed, but if you take a step back for a moment, you will realize that the problem is with the other person, not you. If *they* don't like your shirt, then they won't ask to borrow it! If your haircut is not to *their* liking, too bad. Don't take things personally, just brush it off and move on. The ability to not take things personally and be resilient allows us to continue on our path towards happiness, success, and sanity.

> Don't take things personally.

The quote by Helen Keller at the beginning of the chapter accentuates the importance of being resilient. This quote points out our tendency to allow past mistakes or problems to interfere with future success. We oftentimes dwell so much on things that have gone wrong that we do not even see the new opportunities right in front of us. Being resilient is about making peace with the doors that have closed and allowing ourselves to explore the ones that have newly been opened.

Remember:

- *Resilience: Have the courage and strength to let go of your problems and move on.*
- *Let it go and let it be: don't let the past interfere with your present or future.*
- *Creative visualization: Envision yourself achieving the outcome you desire.*

Chapter 8: Fearlessness

*"You were put on this earth to achieve
your greatest self, to live out your
purpose, and to do it fearlessly."*

*—Steve Maraboli, motivational
speaker and author*

The fifth and final quality that is necessary for thriving throughout the teenage years and living a more meaningful life is *fearlessness*. Whether we realize it or not, fear is a pretty powerful emotion that motivates the majority of our actions or inactions. Fear is what prevents us from doing so many things: fear of the unknown, fear of failure, and fear of being different are just a few examples of the many ways in which fear impacts our lives. Fear is just another form of resistance, and when we fear things, we give them more power than they deserve.

Most adolescents think that being fearless means engaging in risky behaviors, but it is important to understand that fearlessness and recklessness are not the same thing. Being reckless is acting on a whim without much regard for future consequences, while being fearless is having the courage to step out of one's own comfort zone and try new things. Therefore, living fearlessly allows us to open our hearts and minds to new experiences without resistance or judgment. When we are fearless, we allow ourselves to fully indulge in all the rich experiences that life has to offer, rather than being held back by "what ifs" and worries.

Once you have acquired some measure of self-acceptance, compassion, a healthy selfishness, and resilience, you can start to live fearlessly. The key to living fearlessly, however, is sensibility. Sensibility is what separates fearlessness from recklessness: it allows you to view things in a realistic way. While fearlessness allows you to take chances and live beyond the "what ifs,"

> Fearlessness and recklessness are not the same thing.

sensibility will keep you grounded and prevent you from crossing over into recklessness.

Each week when encouraging members of the class to go beyond their comfort zones, my yoga teacher says: "Fear stands for False Evidence Appearing Real." When she says this, people usually laugh and continue with their practice, but I really believe her words to be true. Put simply, fear is a construct of our minds that we convince ourselves is real. Of course there are times when we are in danger and our fear is legitimate, but these are few and far between. In everyday encounters, we often manufacture our own fear and use it as an excuse to avoid change.

We fear the unknown so we choose to ignore the stranger in need. We fear failure so we don't even bother to try something new. We fear being different so we buy the clothes everyone else has in order to blend in. We fear rejection so we don't tell someone else how we really feel. We try to justify all of these things we do on a daily basis by creating "valid" excuses, when in reality we are just scared of change or rejection. Playing it safe is comfortable and may seem like it is working for you, but the truth of the matter is: if you never try, you will never know. The excuses we make are just false evidence that we convince ourselves to be real. We are the ones standing in our own way. We are the ones who create the shackles that bind us. Once we realize that fear *is* our biggest obstacle, we can let go and start to live freely.

Being fearless can be applied to every single aspect of our lives. Whether with academics or social life, almost all of our problems stem from fear. Life is too short to allow our fear to stand in the way of doing what we really want to do and being who we were meant to be. So many people live the majority of their lives motivated by fear, only to wish later on down the road that they had taken more chances, more risks, and lived for themselves. If we start to live fearlessly at a young age, we will create much more authentic lives for ourselves and we will find that we have fewer regrets later in life. Better to have tried and failed than never to have tried at all. If not *now,* when?

A life lived in fear is never really lived at all, so why not put yourself out there? You will regret the chances you never took more than you will regret the mistakes you made, because with the mistakes, you at least know you tried. You stick with what is familiar because you believe that familiarity will help you survive, but who wants to just get by when you have the potential to create a truly extraordinary life for yourself?

All that stands between you and the life that you want is fear. Anxiety, doubt, nervousness, and anger are all merely forms of fear. So, at times when you are experiencing these different forms of fear, ask yourself: "What is the worst that can happen?" Because fear is a construct of our minds, we allow it to run rampant without even questioning whether or not it is warranted.

We think: I feel it, so therefore it must be real! However, if we take a step back and try to make sense of what we are feeling, we can see just how unnecessary it is. For instance, if you are feeling anxious about talking to the boy or girl that you like and fail to let them know how you feel, then you will never know what could have been if you had only had the courage and self-confidence to let them know. There are three scenarios that could occur:

> All that stands between you and the life that you want is FEAR.

1.) He or she will think you're "weird" and will tell everybody how weird you are.

2.) He or she will be flattered but respond that they prefer to be friends.

3.) He or she will feel relief that you had the courage
to approach them and will tell you they feel the
same way.

Regardless of which of these outcomes occurs, it is
still better than doing nothing in fear of rejection. If you
embrace the concept of not taking anything personally, as
discussed in the prior chapter, then the "worst" scenario
is not so bad.

This example demonstrates how much unnecessary
fear we create over simple, everyday encounters. And,
even worse, this fear that we are creating is about things
that haven't even happened yet! Doing this multiple
times a day, every single day of our lives is extremely
pointless, incredibly exhausting, and one-hundred percent
avoidable. Rather than allow the fear to run rampant in
your mind, use some logic when you ask yourself: "What
is the worst that can happen?" You will find that the
majority of the outcomes that you fear will not take place,

and even if one of the outcomes does occur, it really is not that bad. You can't allow an imagined end result of something that hasn't even happened yet to control how you live your life. Otherwise, you will spend your entire life trying to avoid things such as change, rejection, and failure, only to find that you never truly lived for yourself. Familiarity and conformity will allow you to get by and survive, but it is fearlessness that will allow you to live a life of purpose, meaning, and happiness.

Remember:

- *FEAR= **F**alse **E**vidence **A**ppearing **R**eal*
- *Fearlessness: Have the courage to step out of your comfort zone and try new things.*
- *Open your heart and mind to new experiences without resistance or judgment.*
- *Live beyond the "what-ifs."*
- *Ask yourself: "What is the worst that can happen?*

Chapter 9: Calming Techniques

"Breathe. Let go. And remind yourself that this very moment is the only one you know you have for sure."—Oprah Winfrey

Relaxation, Meditation, and Breathing Exercises

In the midst of all the chaos that we experience in our academic, social, and family lives, it is crucial that we find time to take care of ourselves. We spend so much of the day worrying about other people and obligations, and in order to stay sane and healthy it is important to reserve some time for ourselves. Taking time to relax amid all the chaos will help keep us balanced, and can be accomplished through both meditation and breathing exercises.

Meditation

One way to take time for yourself and tune out the stresses of everyday life is through meditation. The practice of meditation is one that is foreign to most teenagers, and people often sneer at this concept simply because they do not know much about it. At the mention of meditation, most people's minds flood with images of people burning incense and sitting cross-legged on the floor while chanting the word "Om." While this vision may be one form of mediation, it is certainly not the only, or most common, way to practice. The style of meditation varies from person to person, and it can be simple, easy, and be practiced almost anywhere.

Meditation has proven to be effective in managing stress; it allows us to feel calmer, as well as view stressful situations in a more objective way. In addition to the emotional benefits of meditation, medical professionals have recognized that meditating can have a positive effect on one's physical health as well. Once we understand the merits of meditation, we can explore different ways of implementing this practice in our everyday lives. Meditation can mean simply taking time out of your day to sit in a quiet place and focus your attention on nothing but yourself, your body, and your mind. If you had a stressful day at school, meditating is an opportunity for you to forget about all of the worries crowding your head and just *be*. When you meditate, you are temporarily leaving all responsibility and reason behind, and allowing yourself to exist only in the present moment. You can get a good look at how much worrying you do just by observing your mind as it thinks. There are many different ways to meditate, and it is important that you find the one that works best for you.

One way to meditate is to sit or lie down in a quiet place and listen to a meditation tape. Some meditation tapes just have soothing music, while others are "guided" by an instructor. If you would rather not use a meditation soundtrack, simply lying on the couch while listening to your own soft music can be helpful in quieting the mind.

Another way to meditate is to sit or lie down in a quiet space, and, instead of listening to music, simply focus on your breath. Sitting quietly and focusing on each inhalation and exhalation can help you shut out the world around you and tune in to the present moment. Make sure your breaths are slow and steady since people tend to take quick and shallow breaths when they are feeling stressed or anxious. Try starting this way: take one deep breath in, and in your mind say: "breathing in." Then, as you exhale, say in your mind: "breathing out." Repeat this until you have a quiet mind, You can start with just five minutes, and then work your way up from there. It's normal for your mind to wander. When, and if, it does, just be patient and start the exercise over again. There is no right or wrong way to meditate, just do what feels right for you to quiet your mind.

Breathing Exercises

Earlier in the book, I mentioned breathing as a tool to use when feeling stressed. In the midst of a stressful situation, stopping to take one deep breath can help us regain composure and approach the situation in a calmer way. In addition to this, there are other ways for us to utilize our breathing in order to relieve tension and calm down.

One exercise that utilizes breathing is called Energy Correction. In this exercise, you take a deep breath while pressing on different parts of your body. Energy Correction can be used when you are feeling anxious, nervous, or overwhelmed to "reset" yourself. It is important to really focus on the exercise while doing it, so that you may restore your body's correct energy balance and feel calmer.

Energy Correction Exercise:

1.) Find a quiet place, close your eyes, and take a deep breath.

2.) Press the left hand on the belly button.

3.) Place the right hand on the crown of your head.

4.) Take a long, slow breath.

5.) Keep the left hand pressed to the belly button while you move the right hand to different parts of the body (see steps below).

6.) Press the right hand to the collarbone and breathe slowly.

7.) Press the right pointer finger flat under the nose and breathe slowly.

8.) Press the right pointer finger flat under the bottom lip and breathe slowly.

9.) Press the top of the right hand against the mid-back (so that the palm faces out) and breathe slowly.

10.) Drop both arms at your sides and take a slow cleansing breath.

Repeat this exercise using the opposite hand, placing your right hand on the belly button and moving the left hand down the body, and so on.

A Final Note

"We are all here for some special reason. Stop being a prisoner of your past. Become the architect of your future."—Robin Sharma

We have now reached the point where our journey draws to a close. After introducing you to new ways of thinking and the five qualities for maintaining sanity, you possess everything you need to handle anything that comes your way with a *new perspective!*

During difficult times, you may find it hard to implement *all* that you have learned but, if you look inside yourself, take a deep breath and smile, you will realize that things are not as bad as they seem. Be patient with yourself, as it takes practice and determination to achieve acceptance, compassion, selfishness, resilience, and fearlessness in your everyday life.

It's time to begin living the life you deserve. May you always be happy, confident, and in control of your own life!

NOTES

NOTES

NOTES